GEESE

BARNYARD FRIENDS

Jason Cooper

The Rourke Book Co., Inc.
Vero Beach, Florida 32964

Edited by Sandra A. Robinson and Pamela J.P. Schroeder

PHOTO CREDITS
All photos © Lynn M. Stone

Library of Congress Cataloging-in-Publication Data

Cooper, Jason, 1942-
    Geese / by Jason Cooper.
    p. cm. — (Barn yard friends)
    Includes index.
    ISBN 1-55916-089-6
    1. Geese—Juvenile literature. [1. Geese. 2. Farm life.]
I. Title. II. Series: Cooper, Jason, 1942- Barn yard friends.
SF505.3.C66   1995
636.5'98—dc20   94-38413
                                                    CIP
                                                    AC

Printed in the USA

TABLE OF CONTENTS

GEESE

Farmers have been raising **domestic,** or tame, geese for thousands of years.

Geese — along with ducks and swans — belong to a group of birds called waterfowl. Like their wild cousins, domestic geese are large, long-necked birds.

Tame geese are much heavier than wild geese. Large geese weigh 25 pounds or more. Domestic geese can only fly a few feet at a time because they weigh so much.

Domestic geese flap their wings, but fail as fliers

WHAT GEESE LOOK LIKE

Domestic geese are smaller than swans but larger than ducks. They have fat bodies with short tails. They waddle on short legs and wide, webbed feet.

Geese wear a "raincoat" of oily, waterproof feathers. Geese have a soft, thick coat of **down** underneath their outer feathers.

Domestic geese may be white or a mixture of gray and brown, depending upon the **breed,** or kind, of goose.

Like bookends, a pair of domestic geese frame their larger cousin — a swan

WHERE GEESE LIVE

Few farmers in North America raise only geese. Most domestic geese live on farms where other animals are also raised. Large goose farms are more common in Europe, where goose meat is a popular food.

Farmers let geese roam around barnyards and pastures. Geese live in coops — special houses for domestic birds — or barns when they need shelter.

On a tour of the farm, a flock of geese preens in the sheep pasture

BREEDS OF GEESE

Long ago, people in Europe and Asia caught and tamed wild greylag and swan geese. These became the first domestic geese.

Over the years, goose farmers picked the geese that they wanted to have babies. By choosing parent geese carefully, farmers were able to raise geese of different colors and types. Each basic type of domestic goose is a breed.

The four most common breeds are the Chinese, Toulouse, African and Embden geese.

Blue-eyed, snow-white Embdens are a favorite breed of American goose farmers

11

An African gander (left) bosses his flock of Toulouse geese

Some farmers raise a heavy, domestic version of these wild Canada geese

WILD GEESE

More than 40 kinds of wild geese live around the world — except on Antarctica.

Wild Canada geese and snow geese are common kinds of wild geese in North America. Some farmers raise domestic Canada geese.

Wild geese are strong fliers. Each spring and fall flocks of wild geese fly long distances. They travel from one feeding or nesting place to another. These long trips are called **migrations.**

14

Hundreds of thousands of wild snow geese migrate across North America each spring and fall

BABY GEESE

Geese lay their eggs in nests of straw or goose down. For about four weeks, the goose keeps her eggs warm by sitting on them. The gander, or male goose, often stands guard nearby.

Goslings, the baby geese, are covered by down. The goslings pop from the nest soon after hatching from their eggs, and follow the mother goose.

Goslings grow quickly. They are fully grown eight weeks after hatching. Some domestic geese live to be 30 years old!

Covered by warm, fuzzy down, goslings leave the nest quickly and follow their mothers

HOW GEESE ARE RAISED

Farmers let geese wander about to graze on grass and other plants. Their short, flat bills have sawlike edges for cutting plant stems. Farmers also feed geese corn and grain.

Domestic geese spend most of their time on land, but they like to paddle around in ponds and streams. Sometimes they dip their heads to snip pieces of underwater plants.

A Toulouse goose grazes in a pasture

HOW GEESE ACT

Barnyard geese stroll from place to place in noisy, honking flocks. A large gander usually bosses the flock.

Domestic geese are usually not afraid of people. A goose may arch its neck, flap its wings and hiss at someone who comes too close.

When they are not feeding or napping, geese **preen** themselves. A goose preens, or cares for its feathers, with its bill. The goose uses its bill to clean, straighten and apply body oil to feathers.

Preening, a Toulouse goose cleans and waterproofs its feathers

HOW GEESE ARE USED

Farmers raise geese for their meat and down. Goose meat is a favorite Christmas treat in Germany and France.

Downy feathers are very soft and warm. Today, goose down is used to fill pillows, mattresses, sleeping bags and parkas. The Romans and early Europeans used goose down more than 2,000 years ago.

In the 1700s, goose feathers were used as **quills,** or feather pens.

Glossary

breed (BREED) — a special group or type of an animal, such as a *Chinese* goose

domestic (dum ES tihk) — referring to any of several kinds of animals tamed and raised by humans

down (DOWN) — a layer of soft, tiny feathers on ducks and geese

gosling (GAHZ ling) — a baby goose

migration (mi GRAY shun) — a long, regular seasonal journey

preen (PREEN) — to carefully clean and oil feathers

quill (KWILL) — the long, hollow stem of a feather